Universities:
Knowing Our Minds

CHATTO
CounterBlasts

Mary
WARNOCK

Universities:
Knowing Our Minds

Chatto & Windus
LONDON

Published in 1989 by
Chatto & Windus Ltd
30 Bedford Square
London WC1B 3SG

A CIP catalogue record for this book
is available from the British Library

ISBN 0 7011 3546 8

Photoset in Linotron Ehrhardt by
Rowland Phototypesetting Ltd
Bury St Edmunds, Suffolk
Printed in Great Britain by
St Edmundsbury Press Ltd,
Bury St Edmunds, Suffolk

WHEN VICTORIAN values ruled and industrial optimism was at its height; when education, both for women and men, seemed the way to a new world, the great universities of Manchester and Leeds, Sheffield, Liverpool and Hull were founded with industrial money, the names of their benefactors perpetuated. There have been great benefactions in the twentieth century too; but as time has gone on, the universities have come to be regarded with increasing indifference. We have now reached the worst possible situation where many of the public, including the wealth-producing public, regard higher education as an irrelevance, while Government, although professing its high-minded goals and benign intentions, in practice regards it with manifest distrust and often with downright hostility. There is little respect for the academic or pride in the intellectual. Whereas the self-made men of earlier times valued the kind of education they had not had, and wanted to ensure it for others, the present controllers of finance, public and private, many of them university-educated, have lost faith in what they themselves enjoyed.

Yet the scale of modern universities is such that

they cannot continue without support from sources other than the fees of their students. The equipment needed for the pursuit of the sciences, the range of material needed in libraries, cannot be compared with what was adequate ninety years ago. Vast private munificence would be needed to keep all this going. There is no realistic alternative to Government support. And so the present hostility towards the universities is a disaster.

We must ask why it is that Government is apparently both ignorant of the function of the universities and, at best, ambivalent in its attitude to them.

In the 1960s the universities became exceedingly unpopular. It was the time of Robbins-led expansion, and, after 1968, of student 'activism' on unattractive French and American models. Students were not only more numerous but more pestilential, radical, dirty and subversive. Their teachers were tarred, not always unfairly, with the same brush, and because the expansion had been so swift, there was an often justified suspicion that many of them were not very bright. At any rate, though times have changed, the general public tends still to think of the universities as the home of idle yobs, interested in nothing but sociological explanations of their own bad behaviour. There is a contradictory myth, too, that students are spoiled socialites, from the pages of *Brideshead Revisited*, their teachers idling their time away with port and cigars. Neither image is endearing. It is tempting to conclude that no public money, or at any rate much less public money, should be committed to the support of such unmeritorious drones.

Mythology apart, the ambivalence of Government stems from a deep confusion about what it wants of the universities. On the one hand they must be in the forefront of teaching and research, technologically sophisticated and entirely up to date; on the other hand they must exist without any increase, and preferably with a steady reduction, in direct funding. Again they must admit more students, in spite of the demographic fall in the number of eighteen-year-olds; but in no circumstances must academic standards decline. We are piously told that the function of the universities is cultural and educational in the widest sense, yet at the same time all departments, even the most abstract and theoretical, are in practice required to show their cost-effectiveness, output measured against input in the manner of a commercial company. Finally, members of the universities are expected to produce top-class work both in teaching and research while suffering from the contempt of Government, a contempt plainly shown by the low level of their salaries compared with those of other professionals and of academics abroad, and by the accusations made at them for being out of touch, inhabitants not of the real world but of that dread place, the Ivory Tower.

The image of the Ivory Tower is of a place of seclusion where everyone, it is implied, might like to live but where most could not afford to, nor would their conscience, practicality and plain common sense permit them to do so. But in speaking of it, in using that particular cliché, there is a hint of rancour, indeed of envy; and it is hard not to suspect an element of disappointed hope in some of the civil servants who, advising ministers and writing their speeches, fuel the flames of hostility. There is too often, clearly audible, the underlying snarl. For there is no doubt that relations between Government and the universities have deteriorated even since the early days of the financial cuts. As a result of its safe and long-lived majority in Parliament, Government feels little need to justify its actions, whether it is dealing with the legal profession, the doctors, or the privatisation of water. In the case of education, now that the Reform Bill has come onto the Statute Book, it seems to believe that the great lines of policy are in place, and all it has to do is proceed as fast as possible to the new Realism. If the universities bring forward objections, they are accused of 'whingeing'. They are reminded that it is 'tax-payers' money' that is being spent on them, and that the receipt of such money is subject to conditions. If they suffer, well, they had it coming to them, after all those years of whooping it up in the Ivory Tower. The barely concealed sense of triumph that the pride of the universities should be brought low makes rational discussion of future policy both difficult and disagreeable.

Yet policy must still be discussed. For though the Education Act deals with all education from primary to higher, there is still enormous confusion about the relation between school and university, or university and other providers of post-school education. Nor is there any hint of recognition that universities have an international as well as a national role. Indeed the only discernible thread running through the Act is that as much of the system as possible should be funded by non-Government sources. And this hardly amounts to a policy. In the same spirit, the newly established University Funding Council, set up to distribute the money allocated by Government to the universities, has as one of its stated aims 'to see that an increasing proportion of the ... incomes of universities should be derived from non-Government sources'. This seems a somewhat perverse aim for a funding council to adopt. And while its adoption is defended in high-sounding phrases about freeing universities from 'dependence' on Government, it is hard – well, impossible – not to think that it means simply that they are to get less public funding. After all, they are never really going to become financially independent of Government, and Government itself neither seriously believes nor wishes that they should. (It is not all that keen, one may think, on the 'independence' of the BBC.)

The fact is that, before it is too late, we must try to reach some kind of agreement on what the universities are actually supposed to do, both in the context of this country and beyond. The conflicting demands made by Government make this a task of urgency.

The strongest thread, then, in Government policy is that universities should become sensitive to the market, and move gradually into profitability, and away from dependence on central funding. So what would this mean? What would it be for a university to be market-led?

As usual, the Government does not seem to have one clear answer to this question. One innovation is that student fees are to be greatly increased, direct funding through the Funding Council being proportionately diminished. This will mean that the more students a university admits, the better off it will be. In the words of Mr Robert Jackson, the Junior Minister in charge of higher education, 'Because a greater proportion of universities' income will depend on the attractiveness of what they are offering, they will have to fix on what is attractive and market it more effectively'. Universities will be in competition with one another for students, and they may hope to pack them in by 'attractive' prospectuses and other marketing devices. In the words of Mr Kenneth Baker, 'with the drop in the number of eighteen-year-olds, heads of institutions will have to go out and market what they have on offer. They will not be able simply to wait for applications to come in'.

Most misleadingly, Mr Baker has referred to this new style of university education as 'the American Model'. He sees it as going along with a large increase in the proportion of the population as a whole attending university or other institutions of higher education, and an increasing independence of those institutions. There is a double confusion here, to which I must digress, in order to remove it. First, there is a suggestion that in America most universities are independent of State funding. This is simply not the case. The largest universities are mostly funded by their States if not by Federal funds; and even the great 'private' universities such as Harvard and Yale are to a large extent in receipt of Government funds. Only some of the small 'Liberal Arts Colleges' are dependent on private endowment and student fees alone, and they, since they deliberately eschew almost the whole of the physical sciences, medicine and engineering, would scarcely serve as a model for universities as a whole. Secondly, many of the institutions called in America by the name 'university' would not be so called in this country. Just as Americans call stones 'rocks' and seas 'oceans', so they call many colleges of further education 'universities', and the diplomas they award 'degrees'. We in this country have some fairly chaotic distinctions within the whole field of post-school education which would be difficult to explain or justify. But, broadly, non-degree-giving institutions are called Colleges, degree-giving institutions either Universities or Polytechnics. In spite of the recent establishment of the Polytechnics and Colleges Funding Council to match the Universities Funding Council, I do not believe that the distinction thus drawn will survive. However there *is* an important distinction, which cuts across this one, namely that between wholly vocational subjects (such as hairdressing or carpentry) and subjects which are either not vocational at all (such as mathematics or medieval history) or are vocational, but with a strong academic content (such as medicine or law). Only the latter two should be studied for a degree, the others for diplomas; (and this is more or less the case at present). In the end I suppose, and hope, that all degree-giving institutions will come under the same Funding Council. But for the time being, when I speak of a University, I refer to an institution currently so called, and funded by the UFC. None of these distinctions is exactly paralleled in America.

Leaving America out of it, we may return to the marketing of university courses to attract students. There appears to be a belief, in Government circles, that if students were encouraged to choose the courses that appealed to them this would, by the operation of some invisible hand, also satisfy the needs of industry and commerce. One component of the so-called 'market', namely potential students, would click neatly into harmony with the requirements of the other end of the 'market', namely potential employers. We in the universities are repeatedly told that we do not 'produce' or 'turn out' enough graduates to satisfy the demands of industry. But it is quite uncertain whether, if we gave students only such courses as they found 'attractive', we should do any better. On the contrary, it might be that most students would end up studying English Literature or Environmental or Biological Sciences, and the shortage of engineers would become even more acute than it is at present. (This did in fact actually happen some twenty years ago, as Lord Dainton found in his report of 1968.) But fashions change; and a more serious objection to the marketing theory of student admission is that it would entirely defeat all efforts to plan the departments in a university, whether with regard to teaching and equipment, or research. The numbers of teachers required, and the spaces in classrooms or laboratories, would be dependent on the whims of those students wishing to apply for admission.

But there is a far more fundamental objection still. Throughout the pronouncements of Government that I have been considering, and basic to all its thinking on the subject, is an obsessive concern with how the universities are to be paid for. One method, as we have seen, is to make students pay higher fees (ultimately by means of loans) and pack more of them in. The content of a university course, or, to put it more realistically, the activities of those employed in the university, are considered only in a secondary way. They will flow from student demand, or from the demands of future employers. At every stage it is someone else, not the academics themselves, who are supposed to determine what is taught, and what subjects are to occupy the minds of the professionals. But this is manifestly back to front. Students can pick what they want to study only from what *is* on offer. They cannot know, they are, so far, too ignorant to know, what *ought* to be on offer. Equally, industrialists may know in broad terms what sort of people they wish to employ. But they cannot know, it is not their business to know, what academic disciplines will ensure that such people will come forward for employment.

Increasing the proportion of funding to be derived from fees is the first novelty. If we turn to the second innovation, the setting up of the UFC, we shall see the same phenomenon. Unlike the University Grants Commission, which it replaces, the UFC exists simply to distribute funds, subject to such conditions as the Secretary of State may determine. It has no advisory function whatsoever. The UGC, on the other hand, had a duty to advise ministers on the needs of universities, and departments within them; and here we see the most significant change. For the concept of a 'need' suggests that there may be goals set up by the universities; and the universities may require support if they are to be able to reach those goals. They might *need* certain grants, *if* they were to be able to do what they aimed to do. But the notion of 'need' has gone, and with it the notion of 'grants'. Instead, the universities will receive money only in exchange for certain services that they are to supply; and what those services are will depend on what the market demands. How much money is paid will presumably also, as in other commercial transactions, depend on the state of the market. The initiative in embarking on particular research or particular courses for students is removed from the universities, and taken over by the other party to the contract.

An optimist might say that things will not really change much. The UFC will continue to fund recognised departments that are seen to have done good work in the past; and undergraduates will continue to study those courses that the universities have always offered. But the strong preference in all Government documents for the language of 'contract' rather than that of 'grant' suggests that such optimism may be misplaced. Moreover Lord Chilver, the first Chairman of the UFC, and formerly Vice-Chancellor of Cranfield Institute of Technology, has made it very clear that in his view the UFC would support only those departments within universities which could satisfy the Council that they had plans to acquire funds from outside sources. Undergraduates and graduate students would pay their own fees, he suggested, though some few who could not do so through loan or sponsorship would be offered 'charity' by the DES.

Fortunately, since October 1988 when he uttered these extraordinary statements, Lord Chilver has learned to keep quiet. But his interview at that time made an indelible impression, especially when he ventured to speculate about how, say, a History department would meet the approval of the UFC. It must, he said, be relevant. For if it were not, students would not choose to study within it; and if it were, it might be able to find outside support, by making historical films or selling its services to museums or television companies. Above all, every such department must be different. If what is on offer is like what is offered by other History departments, 'we shall say we've got enough of those'. It seems that the proper question to ask is not how to do, say, a Modern History course well, but how to do it in some eye-catchingly distinctive way that has not hitherto found favour among serious historians.

To remove from the universities the authority to determine what is taught or what pursued as a subject for research, and place it in bodies outside the university is precisely in line with the rest of the rhetoric of the Ivory Tower. The universities, it is supposed, are not fit to make such decisions, since they are out of touch with reality.

I do not believe, then, that there is much room for optimism. Somehow (but I do not know how), Government must be brought to recognise that universities are, and must remain, the source of those 'academic standards' which, when they are talking about schools, Ministers are so eager to maintain, even improve. This entails that the universities must remain at the top of the educational pyramid, not only in the sense that they are the last ladder-rungs, chronologically, to be attained by those climbing up towards the educational heights, but also in the crucial sense that not everyone will climb up so far. There is, and must always be, an intellectual élite, responsible for innovation and discovery, and the inculcation and preservation of academic standards. And it follows that *what* is provided at university must remain ultimately the responsibility of the universities themselves. Robert Jackson is reported to have said that 'Government will become the customer, not the provider, of higher education'. So be it: but he should also accept that the customer is not always right, and may have to take what he is offered for sale.

One proposal, apparently favoured by Government, is to acknowledge that there exist some academically élite institutions (Centres of Excellence) but to confine these excellent institutions to a research role. Early in 1989, Kenneth Baker said, 'Another traditional value is under challenge. This is the tradition which holds that all teaching at the level of higher education must be accompanied by research at the frontiers of knowledge, and that funding for the universities must be provided on the basis that forty per cent of the time of all academic staff must be devoted to research.' In repudiating this traditional value, he seems inclined to follow the lead of the Advisory Board for the Research Councils who, in 1987, published a paper, *A Strategy for the Science Base*, in which they argued for three levels of universities, the R, the X and the T. 'R' universities should devote themselves entirely to research, and resources should be concentrated in them. Below them would come the 'X' universities, run-of-the-mill establishments, concerned with both teaching and research, and providing taught courses for undergraduates and graduates. At the bottom, there would be some universities which would be devoted wholly to teaching, where Mr Baker would hope there would cluster 'excellent teachers', who could be 'scholars', in the sense that they would keep up with their subjects, though they would not contribute to these subjects. Such universities would not have facilities for research in the sciences, nor would they have first-class libraries. They would presumably be funded entirely by student fees. They would, however, offer their own degrees.

Such a split is proposed on two grounds. First, the provision of research facilities is too expensive to be feasible in all universities; secondly, good teaching is essential to universities, and it is easier to assess teaching if it can be evaluated separately from the evaluation of research.

It may be sensible to fund undergraduate and graduate teaching separately from research. Certainly in estimating the needs of a university department, the proportion of research-time for members of staff need not be assumed to be uniformly forty per cent, as it has been till now. A great deal will depend on the nature of the teaching required in a department, and the number of students within it who may be expected to go on into research themselves and will therefore need gradual access to research resources and techniques. A department of Law, for example, will have fewer such students, as a rule, than will a department of Microbiology. But to say this is not to say that there should be some members of a department expected to *do no research at all*, still less that there should be whole departments, or whole universities, in which research is not funded.

To insist on the necessary connection between teaching and research at university level does not entail that *every* subject must be catered for and pursued at *every* university. The demands of economy may make rationalisation of expensive equipment in the sciences necessary; and the study of certain languages might be confined (as to some extent is the case already) to specific universities. But to suggest that Astronomy might be best concentrated in Cambridge or Chemical Engineering in Bradford or Russian in London, though it may be unpopular with the universities deprived in these subjects, does not carry the implication that some universities should be deprived of *all* the means of research. Such concentration of particular subjects might even work for the good of the system as a whole, spreading prestige, and helping to weaken the domination of the older universities. But this argument is not the same as the argument for a distinction between 'Teaching' and 'Research' universities. Equally, the criteria of assessment of teaching and of research, related to funding, may perfectly well be different, without the consequence that the activities should be carried out in different institutions.

The funding and the assessment of teaching

and research may, then, be totally separate; but to suppose that the two activities are not inevitably connected seems to show an amazing ignorance (or forgetfulness) of what a university is, and what its function must be. The crucial distinction between university and other forms of education lies simply in its necessary connection with research. For at school, sixth-form college or college of higher education, however good teachers may be, they are generally teaching the received wisdom in their subject. They may be critical of this wisdom; they may hold unorthodox or eccentric views. But it is very unlikely that they will themselves be engaged in discovering new things or publishing reasoned objections to orthodox thinking. They are unlikely to have either the time or the resources to enable them to enter new fields. More important, as teachers, their main task will be to help their students to get on to the next stage, and to pass examinations based on the 'received' view of the subject-matter. If they do anything else, they fail in their duty. Thus the school teacher, who is nothing but a teacher, is inevitably part of a conservative system, academically speaking.

At university, on the other hand, the student should become aware of a profound difference. Even if not all the student's teachers are engaged in innovatory research, they may be presumed to be in touch through colleagues with such research.

Students should realise, as part of their university experience, that their teachers are not primarily interested in them, but, just as much, in their own subject. University pupils, simply through being taught, can help in the advancement of the subject. I do not deny the need for excellent teachers in universities; and if there are those who are bad, we should seek to remedy this. But being a 'good teacher' is not something which, at university, *can* ever be wholly separated from the advancement of learning, even in the case of those teachers who do not publish much themselves. The number of publications to the credit of a university employee will never be a sure guide to his or her excellence, either as an innovator or as a teacher. The test is that students, even undergraduate students, should be conscious through their teachers of standing on the edge of a developing and changing world of learning. They may attend lectures and seminars where innovations are being made in front of their very eyes and ears. It is not simply that they will be told about them; they may in some measure take part in them. Even the syllabus which they follow, though on paper it may be the same as it was last year and the year before, may in fact be evolving, in line with the changes that are coming about on their own doorstep, as a result of the work done by the very people who are teaching and examining them. To be the pupil of an intellectual innovator is to take part, albeit indirectly, in the innovation itself. It is an experience which, more than any other, expands the imaginative horizons.

I do not, then, deny the right of Government, through the UFC, to concentrate its expensive research in particular universities. If Government has a duty, as I believe, to support research in universities, it also has a right to determine the limits of that support. The university system as a whole cannot defend the right of each and every member of the system to claim funds for whatever it chooses. Universities must, instead, learn to think of themselves as parts of an intellectual *community*, within which there should be easy movement and easy communication. For this very reason, it would be disastrous to formalise a pecking-order within the university system in such a way that at one end there would be universities aiming at nothing but efficient teaching. For the question would have to be raised: *what is it that these universities are teaching so efficiently?* And the answer would have to be, 'the arts and sciences at an elementary level'. As soon as this was clearly recognised, then the standard both of students and teachers at those universities would sink, and the degrees offered would cease to be comparable with other degrees. In this way, the gap between good and less good universities would become fixed and unbridgeable; and this would be bad for higher education as a whole, bad for the intellectual community, and bad for the international standing of our universities.

So whether or not research and teaching are funded and assessed separately, whether or not some specialisation of research-centres is introduced, we *must* presume that all universities will retain both teaching and research facilities. Wherever there is teaching there must be research. Only thus can universities fulfil what they promise, to offer to their students the most academic and intellectual form of higher education, in an imaginative and constantly developing way.

This does not mean, however, that they should be indifferent to demands for more open access. If a greater proportion of the population is expected to enter higher education, including the universities, by the end of the century, this means that a wider variety of potential students must come forward, from more various backgrounds, with more various experience, and of more various ages. The universities must do everything in their power to share in this pool of new students and to benefit them. To say this is quite different, of course, from suggesting that the universities should, like comprehensive schools, be open to people of all abilities. If universities are to fulfil their proper function, they must remain academically selective, just as grammar schools were, in the days of scholarships or the 11+. We must not confuse social with academic egalitarianism. The universities must hope that gradually the bias in their entry towards the middle classes will diminish as school education improves and the expectations of school-leavers rise, especially among women. But much as they must hope for this outcome and do their best to encourage it, they must do nothing to disturb their position as the most academic of the degree-giving institutions, worthy of national and international respect.

And so the aim of the universities can never be to follow the market, in the sense of offering for sale whatever it is that students want. Prospective students often do not know what they want, and certainly do not know what, in order to achieve academic goals, they ought to be given. On the contrary, universities must try to remedy the inability to make intelligent choices, forced upon people by their position in the market economy. They must attempt, by means of what they offer, to lift people out of the limitations, both intellectual and imaginative, in which they have hitherto been bound. And this they must do by a selection procedure and a teaching system which gives equal opportunities to those who present themselves as candidates.

There are two essential ways forward towards such equality of opportunity. First, universities must become more flexible and cooperative in their dealings with schools. Things have no doubt improved a bit since the days when schools, suspecting snobbery and bias, regarded universities (some at least) with naked suspicion. It is more widely recognised now that universities try to be fair, not favouring particular kinds of schools or kinds of candidates. The old-boy network is more or less dead. Nevertheless there is some justice in the complaint that the universities still expect more than some schools feel confident of being able to deliver, especially in the matter of A level grades. This is not surprising, as long as universities are compared with one another according to the A level grades of the candidates they accept. But it is becoming increasingly unrealistic to select students according to A level grades and increasingly absurd to judge the academic standard of a university by the achievements in a school examination of the candidates who are admitted. In the first place, to demand exceptionally high grades favours the independent schools, which can teach for A levels in smaller classes, or give their pupils more special help than can the maintained schools. Secondly, A levels are only moderately good indicators of how well students will perform at university, and how much they will get out of higher education. Thirdly, A levels themselves are in the process of change, since the introduction of the GCSE. One way or another, there will undoubtedly be considerable development in the sixth-form curriculum in schools of every kind, and the universities must interest themselves seriously in such changes, learn to understand them and adapt to them. At present too many university teachers are profoundly ignorant of schools and school education, and have neither time nor inclination to remedy their ignorance.

There is a curious silence about all this from the Government. In 1987, Kenneth Baker set up the Higginson Committee to look into ways in which the A level examination might remain as a 'standard of excellence' ensuring 'breadth and balance of knowledge and understanding . . . without sacrificing depth of study'. (Quite a trick.) When Higginson reported in 1988, the main recommendation was that A levels should be substantially modified. They should become much closer to the GCSE in style, with a wider range of subjects to be studied by each candidate, and different methods of assessment, including assessment by course-work. The report was immediately rejected by Government, for undisclosed reasons and with virtually no discussion. Thus old-fashioned A levels, with the uneasy addition of AS level, as a half-hearted attempt at breadth, remain the norm for sixth-form studies, and universities may still demand grades as high as they please, in a concentration of related specialist subjects, though the GCSE has made it more difficult for candidates to perform well in old-fashioned

A levels. The full effect of this, in combination with the drop in the numbers of eighteen-year-olds, has yet to be seen.

It is essential that universities should now show initiative in the matter of admissions. Students should increasingly be admitted on the basis of their school (or work) record, combined with an undertaking to attend a pre-entry course at the university itself. Such courses should last a month, fees for them should be part of students' overall fees, to be repaid if they do not complete the course. In this month, students should receive intensive teaching to familiarise them both with aspects of the subject they would not have covered at school, and with the general method and outlook of the university. It is astonishing how much can be taught in a month to those who are motivated to learn, and who have a specific goal in mind. The goals would vary between one subject and another, but would all be attainable by a keen student with an energetic teacher. It should be a regular part of the duties of a university teacher to devise and, where possible, teach such courses. It would be good for members of the university to have to present the elements and methodology of their subject; and it would be good for them to experience the weaknesses and strengths of pupils straight from school, or from a different background. There already exist a number of courses of this introductory kind. They should become a regular feature of university entry; and, given sympathy between schools and universities, I do not think there would be many failures to complete.

The second response to the demand for more open access is more radical. There should be a gradual change in the content of university courses themselves. This does not entail a 'lowering of academic standards', but rather, a shift of emphasis. At present a fair amount of knowledge is presumed at the beginning of most university courses, especially in the sciences and modern languages (hence the insistence on A level grades). If asked whether they could accept students who knew less, university teachers are inclined to say they could not, because such students would never be able to 'keep up'.

This is a manifestly question-begging answer. It assumes that more and more knowledge is to be piled on top of whatever exists, and that a student could not assimilate it if he or she started from a lower base. It is sometimes alleged that the only way to 'maintain standards' if students came to university with less knowledge would be to introduce four-year courses, in the Scottish manner (for there as a rule pupils start university earlier, and after a more general sixth-form course). But, apart from the fact that more four-year courses would meet with inevitable disfavour on grounds of expense, it is a gross mistake to think of university education in this quantitative way. We should lay far more emphasis on methods of acquiring knowledge than on retaining it; on understanding and applying principles than on recalling information. This is the direction in which undergraduate curricula (perhaps especially in the sciences) should move. After all, information quickly goes out of date. What is important is for students to grasp enough of their subject to appreciate what is new, to distinguish the probable from the improbable, the well-argued from the wild guess, the properly supported from the phoney. They must understand enough of the principles of what they are studying to see how it connects with other subjects, with which they are less familiar. This method entails a certain amount of detailed knowledge: but a limited amount. It entails what may loosely be called a 'philosophical' approach to the subject.

In every field, this sort of understanding is what distinguishes an educated person from an amateur. Graduates are, or should be, trained to be critical, both of their own ideas and of other people's, not to go off wildly after a bright thought, without finding out whether someone else had it before, or where it might lead. Obviously in their three years of study undergraduates will pick up a good deal of knowledge and retain some of it (and the more interested they become, the more they will retain).

30

But it should be recognised that this retention of knowledge is only a small part of what they are supposed to get from their course. Nearly everyone who has ever been at a university, and most people who have taught in one, admit that it is not *knowledge acquired* but the *underlying mental discipline* that is important. Yet when it comes to admission procedures or the devising of courses, those within the system are reluctant to rely on such insights. If we are to see genuinely wider access to the top of the educational pyramid, then this must change. And it could change without our ever deviating from that pursuit of the academic which is the purpose of university education.

The universities, then, must change, and adapt to the new kind of student they will have. Retaining academic credibility does not mean keeping for ever within the limits of curricula deemed adequate in the past. Government, on its side, has a duty to make up its mind about the nature and function of the universities. The longer it continues to make incompatible demands of the universities, the longer it continues to accuse them of failing to fulfil a function which in truth is not theirs, the deeper the hostility becomes between the universities and those who, for everyone's sake, should support them.

It is not that Government thinking is wrong when it insists that university education should be useful.

From the very earliest days, when the role of universities was to turn out men who could read and write fluently and understand Latin, it has been recognised that there are 'useful' purposes which universities can properly be expected to serve. Rather, to define the role of the universities at the present time, we must rethink the concept of the useful. University students are members of society, and utility must be thought of as the good both of students and of society as a whole; and essentially as a long-term good. All education, at whatever level, is in one sense utilitarian, in that it is undertaken not for its own sake here and now, but for the sake of the future. The *outcome* of education must be shown to be good, whatever its subject-matter. So it is essential that we should abandon the common view that the sciences are useful, looking to the future, and the humanities useless, looking only to the past, or to the pleasures and enjoyment of the education-process itself. For one thing, many of the subjects classed as scientific are not *immediately* applicable, or capable of being exploited directly in the job-market. Members of Government, often themselves educated in the humanities, tend to overlook this fact. They do not understand the vast difference between theory and application, and they fail to recognise the highly abstract and theoretical nature of many science subjects (including engineering science). They link science with technology, and forget the difference between the *use* of technological skills, and the *theoretical* understanding of technology.

In industry, innovation has generally come about when there is a need, identified by the market, for a particular kind of product, which has then come into existence to fill a gap. Universities sometimes have a part to play in such invention; but it is just as likely to come about in the research and development department of the particular industry involved. The Research and Development arm of industry badly needs to be supported, and it needs well-educated science graduates working in it. But such graduates may well be more efficient if they are broadly rather than narrowly educated at university. They cannot be expected to come straight from university already understanding what the particular industry needs, or what the market demands. For to understand this is part not of education but of experience. In contrast, the science departments of universities must be devoted both to general teaching and to pure research, which may or may not ultimately lead to industrial spin-off. In the long run society will benefit from pure research. But no time-limit can be placed on such benefits. And it is too much to demand of a company, intent both on improving its position in the competitive world and on encouraging investors, that it should spend large sums on the kind of research that may have no quick return and that may benefit other companies as much as itself. The great charitable trusts, such as the Wellcome Foundation, not interested in immediate outcomes, may continue to support research in universities. But Government must realise that fundamental scientific research cannot be completely or adequately supported by outside funding. It has to be the responsibility of Government itself.

Still less is it possible to rely on outside funding for the humanities. Yet it would be impossible to conceive of a university system not devoted in part to the pursuit of learning and scholarship in the humanities and to teaching in these fields. We should not rely only on arguments from history and tradition, powerful though these arguments are, in defending the humanities. Instead, we must continue to rethink the 'useful' in education, and see whether gradually Government may be persuaded to support the humanities on utilitarian grounds.

Bernard Williams has argued that to study the humanities is as useful as to study the sciences. He deprecates what he refers to as the 'leather blotter from Harrods' theory of the arts subjects, something to give people when no *useful* gift can be found, no more than a species of conspicuous wealth. Instead Williams suggests that arts subjects are in fact a kind of science, social science, and that they offer a 'truthful understanding of where we are and where we come from such as is indispensable to those who govern'. In a democratic society, he argues, it is essential that such an understanding should be widely spread. It is not an optional extra, to be confined only to an élite or self-indulgent minority.

I believe we should defend the humanities on a wider front, and thus extend still more widely the concept of the 'useful' in education. For, as I have suggested, if we raise the question what are the characteristics of university graduates that we value most, the answer must be in terms not of particular skills nor of the ability to address particular problems, but of a *general* cast of mind. Given that universities will continue to select their students (admittedly from a wider pool), they should select them and educate them on the basis that imagination, critical insight, and the ability to relate one subject to another are the most important attributes of a graduate. Moreover in a democratic society, increasingly and properly demanding the right to understand, one must add the ability to explain issues, both narrow problems and wider implications, to people not themselves experts in a field, but with a legitimate interest in it. Thus a study of the humanities is of the most crucial importance in education at all levels, simply because it is language-based, and offers the chance of practice in clear expression and logical analysis.

Relying, then, on the concept of language, it is possible on the one hand to find a quite narrowly utilitarian justification for the teaching of the humanities in universities: first, for the development of a pool of potential managers capable of communication, and of grasping general principles, and trained in the skills of analysis. These are skills which everyone would agree are needed in management. Secondly, for the development of a body of people who understand the importance of teaching in schools, and handing on standards of clarity and intelligibility to their pupils. But on the other hand it is also possible, and I believe of the greatest importance, to take a wider view still. All of our knowledge must be filtered to us, and passed on by us, through the medium of language. It is essential that there should be those, philosophers, theologians, literary critics, linguists and linguisticians, who are trained to think critically about the relation between language and the world, and between one language and another. It is only through the use of language that we can think coherently and in general terms about either the past or the future. The demand that, above all others, must be met by the universities is that they should release people from what Sir Keith Thomas has called the tyranny of present-mindedness. It is easy for the scientist involved in the immediate problems of teaching and research, easy even for the arts student, brought up at school amid the fashionable jargon of 'problem-solving', to forget that the form in which a problem is set *could* be otherwise. There might be different ways to describe phenomena, different responses to the familiar and the given. The past need *not* be a guide to the future; the immediate and the present is always capable of being reinterpreted. It is the possibility of envisaging a future different from either past or present that lies at the heart of the human imagination. And, without imagination, we should neither be able to succeed as industrialists, nor understand our own environment, ecological, social or political. It must be the expansion of imagination that is the first demand on the universities. This must be accepted as the most useful of all possible outcomes of both teaching and research; and this is also why the universities must remain at the top of the pyramid of education.

If we reject the view, then, that the universities should be primarily concerned with immediately applicable knowledge, it is clear that it would be wrong to expect them to be funded to any great extent by industry. For the aim of imaginative understanding is a perfectly general and democratic aim, which must be a matter of national policy, not of industrial interest. Industry must be concerned to increase its own profitability, if necessary at the expense of other companies. But a general purpose of developing the imagination of students for the common good has nothing to do with competition: it is an essentially egalitarian aim. As such it is a proper concern of the democratic state.

It is common Government rhetoric, today, to assert that the universities should become 'independent'. By this they mean independent of Government, and it sounds good. For who wants universities that are dominated by the state? But there is yet one more fundamental confusion here. For if universities are to be independent of Government, in the sense of being independent of Government *support*, then they must be supported, directly or indirectly, by industry. And the pressures likely to be imposed by industry, demanding instant applicability, overt value-for-money, and perhaps control over the publication of research, are likely to be far more damaging than any pressure from Government. If Government is the paymaster, it may properly demand that the universities be economical, that they demonstrate their good practice and be accountable for the expenditure of funds. Yet they may be free to pursue learning and research that has no short-term utility. Government, unlike industry, has no reason to demand *only* what will show a quick profit. For the universities conceived as intellectual power-houses, the think-tanks to out-think all others, can be regarded as long-term investment, the source of national and international credibility and pride, in the not necessarily calculable future.

It is almost unbelievable that the notion of intellectual investment should be so little considered by the present Government. It is not a novel or a difficult idea. Indeed the phrase 'investing in our future' was an educational cliché in the 1940s, and no doubt before. Yet we hear little of it today. It is true that universities are being urged to spread the benefits of education more widely, and will do so. But the new equality of opportunity is not something that Government is prepared to pay for. Instead, the new students are supposed to pay for themselves. They are supposed not to be able to benefit from their education unless they have to make sacrifices to achieve it, learning, alongside their physics and chemistry, the art of living on money they have borrowed, and will have to repay. The folly of this is that not only will it make the desired spread of university education far more difficult but it will deter those who take degrees from entering the very professions, especially teaching, which have to be filled by the new graduates, if the new academic standards are to be maintained. For who could voluntarily enter the teaching profession burdened by debt? A teacher will almost certainly be in debt anyway, within a year or two, if he or she wishes to buy a house or start a family. If Government recognises the status of the

universities as *academic assets*, it should also recognise its obligation to support them, and those
students who are part of them.

The refusal to see this is based on more than a
simple desire to save money. It stems from a deep
dislike of the intellectual. Despite the avowed desire
that academic standards should be improved at
school, once school is over the academic at once
becomes an object of suspicion and ridicule. For
what is intolerable to politicians is the fact that high
intellectual standards inevitably lead to intellectual
freedom. The dislike felt by Government for the
academic does not stem from philistinism, as is
often supposed, but from dogmatism. To a dogma-
tist, nothing is so horrible as freedom of thought.

I do not believe that there either could or should
be *absolute* academic freedom, if that is taken to
mean that academics should, at their own option,
be protected and indulged in whatever ploys they
may choose to undertake. Universities have com-
promised the true case for freedom by claiming too
much in its name. They cannot expect simply to set
their own terms and write their own cheque. I do
not hold that members of academic staffs should
be immovably entrenched in their jobs for life even
if, for example, their departments are dismantled
or they are proved to be incompetent. Nor, in
general, do I hold that universities are entitled to
dispose of their funds in absolutely any way they

see fit. If Government has a duty to supply the funds, it has a duty also to ensure the responsibility of the universities in spending them. But one may accept this responsibility without eroding the principle of freedom.

The ideal of academic freedom is concerned with the *content* of what is taught, and with the *subject-matter* of research and its publication. It will be when the UFC begins to withdraw support from departments on the basis of the nature of the work they are engaged in that fears for academic freedom will be justified. For it is absurd to suppose that someone else, not the historians, should dictate to the historians what is a proper subject to be taught in their departments, or how they ought to teach it. A philosopher cannot be subject to the judgment of a committee, no single one of whom may have the faintest idea what philosophy is.

In saying this I shall seem to be displaying the arrogance and failure to engage with the Real World that is the very point complained of. But the matter is of the greatest importance.

The universities certainly stand at one end of a continuum of educational provision, starting at nursery school, which is organised and to a large extent provided by Government. But they must not be seen only as the last of the institutions in which people may be educated. A National Curriculum at school is not objectionable, for Government may, within reason, be entitled to demand that school-children should be brought up to a certain level of education, as a minimum. But with universities it is different: they must be seen as the *source* of new knowledge, the *origin* of that critical, undogmatic, imaginative examination of received wisdom without which a country cannot be expected to have its voice heard, and from which ultimately all intellectual standards flow. It is this critical and imaginative function that is in danger, if civil servants and Ministers show themselves unable to accept the intrinsic *authority* of the learned, the academic and the scholarly.

There is nowhere else that such intellectual authority can come from but the universities themselves. This is an area where the concept of the free market is simply not applicable. The universities may gradually influence the market; they cannot be subject to its immediate demands. This is the fact that Government must face, over the next decade. It must make up its mind, and require of the universities *only* what they can properly give, and *all* of that.

It is a depressing thought that in the 1930s great scholars from Europe were welcomed into British universities as honoured refugees, admired, even if their subjects were not useful. It is not certain that in the present dogmatic climate those giants of classical scholarship, Momigliano and Pfeiffer, Maas and Fraenkel would be accorded such protec-

42

tion and respect. If they would not, this is a cause for shame. There have been times, in the memory of some of us, when scholarship and pure research were deemed to be intrinsically good, and a source of pride. Somehow the present Government must grasp such concepts again, and come to understand what the universities are, and what they must be allowed to do. From Government recognition, a general recognition would follow. In a democratic society, we cannot allow the universities to be despised, for it is from the universities that democratic freedom of thought will ultimately find its support.

About the Author

MARY WARNOCK was fellow of St Hugh's College, Oxford from 1950–1966, Headmistress of Oxford High School from 1966 until 1972 and has been Mistress of Girton College, Cambridge since 1985. She is author of *Ethics Since 1900*, *Imagination*, *Memory* and *A Common Policy for Education*.

CHATTO
Counter*Blasts*

Also available in bookshops now:-

No. 1 Jonathan Raban   **God, Man & Mrs Thatcher**
No. 2 Paul Foot   **Ireland:** Why Britain Must Get Out
No. 3 John Lloyd   **A Rational Advance for the**
                        Labour Party
No. 4 Fay Weldon   **Sacred Cows:** A Portrait of Britain,
                        post-Rushdie, pre-Utopia
No. 5 Marina Warner   **Into the Dangerous World**
No. 6 William Shawcross   **After the Massacre**
No. 7 Ruth Rendell   **Undermining the Central Line**
        and Colin Ward

Forthcoming Chatto Counter*Blasts*

No. 9 Sue Townsend   **Mr Bevan's Dream**
No. 10 Christopher   **The Monarchy**
        Hitchens

Counter*Blasts* to be published in 1990 include:-

Tessa Blackstone on prisons and penal reform
Douglas Dunn on Poll Tax
Ludovic Kennedy on euthanasia
Adam Mars-Jones on Venus Envy
Adam Lively on sovereignty
Margaret Drabble on property and mortgage tax relief
Ronald Dworkin on a Bill of Rights for Britain

Plus pamphlets from Michael Holroyd, Harold Evans, Hanif Kureishi, Michael Ignatieff and Susannah Clapp

If you want to join in the debate, and if you want to know more about **Counter*Blasts*,** the writers and the issues, then write to:

Random House UK Ltd, Freepost 5066, Dept MH, London WC1B 3BR